Be True to You
Celebrating the Things that Make Us Unique

I Love my HEART
WilliamT Byrd

A project of the K-Town Youth Empowerment Network Youth Council in collaboration with Knoxville, Tennessee's 2010-2011 Sarah Moore Greene Elementary School's Third Grade Classrooms

K-TOWN
YOUTH EMPOWERMENT NETWORK
www.ktownyouthempowerment.org

Substance Abuse and Mental Health Services Administration
✗SAMHSA
www.samhsa.gov • 1-877-SAMHSA-7 (1-877-726-4727)

MELTON HILL MEDIA

Melton Hill Media, Oak Ridge, Tennessee

ISBN 978-0-9816793-1-0

K-Town Youth Empowerment Network is supported by a
grant from the Substance Abuse and Mental Health Services
Administration (SAMHSA) Center for Mental Health Services,
and Tennessee Department of Mental Health.

Published by   Designed by
Melton Hill Media, LLC   Foursquare ConsultingGroup, LLC
9119 Solway Ferry Road   144 E. Okllahoma Ave.
Oak Ridge, TN 37830   Knoxville, Tennessee 37917
865-803-2286   865.540.1338

wendy@meltonhillmedia.com   jlfuson@4square.ws
www.meltonhillmedia.com   www.4square.ws

Second Edition: *July, 2011*

11-014/12

Foreword

I am grateful that so many people, organizations, and schools across Tennessee show continued commitment to helping children and families to be healthy, safe, and educated. In my years in Knoxville, I have known and worked with many great organizations that are committed to this goal, and Sarah Moore Greene Elementary is among them.

In addition to education, I believe that confident students and youth mentorship can be a very powerful mechanism for change. To everyone involved in this project, you should take great pride in the finished product.

To the K-Town Youth Council members: you are heroes.

It takes incredible strength to look beyond our own struggles to help better the life of someone else. You served as classroom mentors, encouraged strengths in younger students, and talked with children about issues that they were facing at school and at home. Thank you for your commitment to the next generation.

To the Sarah Moore Greene Elementary 3rd grade students: The essays you wrote are more than words on a page—they are a message that every person matters, every person has value, and every person has unique qualities that make them special.

Crissy Haslam

"It takes incredible strength to look beyond our own struggles to help better the life of someone else. "

Tennessee First Lady Crissy Haslam

About K-Town

K-Town Youth Empowerment Network is a community partnership of local agencies, schools, faith-based organizations, government, businesses, youth leaders, and families working together to provide a "System of Care" for Knox County, Tennessee

K-TOWN
YOUTH
EMPOWERMENT
NETWORK

youth ages 14–21 with serious emotional and behavioral challenges, as well as their families. Systems of Care, which operate in nearly

For more about K-Town Youth Empowerment Network

and Systems of Care, please visit our web site, www.ktownyouth empowerment.org.

100 communities nationwide, are coordinated networks of community-based services and supports organized to meet the challenges of youth and families with complex needs. K-Town Youth Empowerment Network is supported by a six-year grant from the Substance Abuse and Mental Health Services Administration (SAMHSA) Center for Mental Health Services. The grant is administered by the Tennessee Department of Mental Health in partnership with Tennessee Voices for Children, Helen Ross McNabb Center, and Centerstone Research Institute. Without the vision and support of these organizations, and our dozens of local community partners, this project would not have been possible.

Dedication

To the parents, educators, counselors, mentors, and advocates who see our potential and work every day to help us maximize it

This project was

a collaborative effort. We are grateful for the individuals and organizations who have contributed to its completion and its success.

Acknowledgements

We recognize and thank the staff of Sarah Moore Greene (SMG) Elementary School, who allowed the Youth Council to present and work with their students to produce the essays and artwork featured in this book. Special thanks to SMG's Principal George Ana Yarbro and third grade teachers Lou Ann Magden, Ruby McClain, Melanie Norsworthy, Carol Giles, Laura Carawan, Rachel Reyes, and Kimberly Watkins. We thank Mrs. Watkins for her vision and for serving as our liaison, helping to coordinate the collaboration.

We offer our deepest gratitude to Melton Hill Media, and J. Lynn Fuson of Foursquare Consulting Group, for offering their time, resources, and expertise in the design, layout, and publishing of this book. Special thanks to Wendy Besmann, K-Town's Social Marketer, who helped bring this project through production.

We are most grateful to Tennessee First Lady Crissy Haslam for her continued efforts on behalf of Tennessee's youth and families, and for contributing the foreword.

Finally, we thank the entire staff of K-Town Youth Empowerment Network for their encouragement and for championing this project.

—Mark Wolf
Project Director
K-Town Youth
Empowerment Network

Introduction

In January 2011, a group of youth advocates in Knoxville, Tennessee, met for pizza and dialogue. They decided to use their voices to make a difference. Their vision was simple: a community where all people are accepted for who they are; where our differences connect us rather than divide us. Equipped with their individual experiences and their stories, they formed the K-Town Youth Empowerment Network Youth Council. The council is united around this core belief:

Every person has unique gifts, talents, and abilities. To maximize our individual potential, we must love ourselves and be confident in who we are.

When we love ourselves, we are more capable of understanding and appreciating others.

Council member and University of Tennessee student, Alexandria Neverson, led the charge to build this message into a public awareness campaign, which the council entitled *"Love Me, Love You."* Council members embraced the mission of carrying this message throughout the community, educating others about developing self-esteem, building confidence, practicing acceptance

"Be True to You: Celebrating the Things that Make Us Unique" Book Project

K-Town Youth Council Members who participated in this project (in alphabetical order): Chris Ball (photography), Shyteshia Gant, William Garnette (art and essay editing), Ramel Gilliam, Genesis Hardin (photography), Paulette Johnson, Jonathan Peak, Aneja Raiteri, and Kelvin Tucker.

and respect, and valuing individuality and diversity.

In March 2011, the staff and students of Sarah Moore Greene (SMG) Elementary School's third grade opened the doors to their classrooms, providing a supportive and attentive audience for the members of the K-Town Youth Council and the "Love Me, Love You" campaign. Youth advocates spoke before the SMG third grade, sharing their experiences and encouraging students to be themselves, to do their best, and to respect one another and the adults in their lives who will help them succeed. Council members served as classroom mentors, listening to students as they shared their own struggles, talents, and triumphs. Mentors encouraged the students to write out their answers to three questions:

What do you love most about yourself?

What are you most proud of?

What do others appreciate most about you?

The students' inspiring, entertaining, and insightful answers to those questions, along with reflections and photography from members of the youth council, form the pages of *Be True To You.* As you read their words, mostly in their handwriting, with their illustrations, we hope you will celebrate the things that make each of them special and that you'll reflect on the things that make each of us uniquely human.

In April 2011, youth advocates met again for pizza and dialogue. This time they talked about the their experiences during the Love Me, Love You campaign. Council member Andy Derthick remarked, "It's about linking the chain. Each of us is a link, but the chain is only strong when all of our pieces are connected." The council and their K-Town facilitators hope that Be True to You will help "link the chains," reminding us to  celebrate the things that make us unique, while encouraging us to strengthen the bonds that keep us united.

This is our story.

Chrystal D. Armstrong

—**Chrystal D. Armstrong**
K-Town Youth
Empowerment
Network Youth and
Cultural and Linguistic
Competency Coordinator

Youth Council members presenting, planning, and partnering with SMG students.

"What I learned from this is experience is that kids are special in different ways. Some of the kids love to draw, or write, or both. I also learned that these kids look to someone older than them for an example. As a child, you often want to be like someone else, but today, I can encourage kids to be themselves, and to love themselves."

–Youth Advocate Kelvin Tucker, 18

Each of us has an unique appearance and we love the way we look.

"When we went to the school, there were so many children touched because they felt unloved. One little boy told me that he feels like no one loved him so I explained, 'if you'll be yourself, you will always have someone by your side.' They made me really thank God for making me special and one of a kind. Walking out of the doors of Sarah Moore Greene made me feel like a better person because I was able to leave a footprint on someone's life."

—Youth Advocate Paulette Johnson, 14

I love my eyes. They are brown and so sweet. I see a lot with my pretty pretty eyes. Every boy and girl is beautiful to see, but now I see I am very beautiful. On the inside I feel glad I'm alive. If I were not around I don't know what mom would do without me.

DeNaizah Smith

What I like about myself is that I am Pretty just the way I am from my hair to my eyes from my eyes to my smile. I like the way I am all around

by: Kayla McNeil

11-014/002_r1

My face
By Kyla Elizabeth Bourne

What I Love about me is my face. One day I had bumps on my face. Everybody Picked on me even my frineds, my mom even my dad. And when my bumps went away everbody stopped Picking on me. Then everbody said I Look Like my cousin and my grandmother. They allways says "Is that your sister? Went my cousin picks me up. And when my grandmother Picks me up they says "Is that your sister"? And until this day nobody I mean nobody is picking on me anymore.

11-014/004

What I Love about me is my eyes. My eyes are beacatiful. My eyes are black. I love my eyes. They are cute. My eyes are nice. My eyes are little, but my eyes are nice to have. I like my eyes just the way they are.
Marresha Mobley

What I like about myself is my eyes. They are a really pretty brown color and in the light they shine. I thank God that I have them. When I look in the mirror, I look deep into my eyes. I stare until I laugh. It's funny because I keep challenging myself, but that's just me.

Nariah Taylor

I love my face a lot. So I don't look ugly and I look good. So I cannot get hurt easily. And I look good at skateboarding. For example, I think I have the best on Earth/America. My face is a very good face and is a beautiful face. People made fun of me. I forgot about it. My friends Derrick, John, and Jalon helped me and say my face is a cool face.

by Christian M. Guinn

What I love about myself is that I'm good at writing and running too. The help me write are my hands and to help me run are my legs. Some other things I love about my self is to darw and to read. To help me darw are my hands and to help me read are my eyes and my brain.

Jalen   Age. 8

What I love about me
I have a great smile. It is very white. It makes
me happy because I brush them every day and night.
I think you should too. One other thing is that
I stay healthy because I eat lots of grains.
I think you should too.

11-014/007

My favorite thing about myself
is my mouth. I like my mouth
becuse it helps me sing. I also
like my feet and hands because I
helps play sports. I love myself!
Mykenzie age 9

What I love most about myself is my hair. I love how it's brown and short. I also how you can put it up almost any way. I'm glad I have my brown hair. It would be hard to live without it. It helps to have my hair. I wouldn't want to have any other kind of hair. People will say it's ugly, but I ignore them. Because I love my hair thats all that matters. If someone asked what do you think is the most beautiful thing on your body, I would say my hair.

Justyce age 8

I really love my arms and legs.
   MY arms and legs can Help
 Me play a basket ball game
and a foot ball game.
 MY arms and legs help me jump
and catch the balls I really
LoVE my arms and legs.
   Steven age 9

I am cute, I am sweet, as a
fruit. From head to toe, from my
smile to my face, I am beautful.

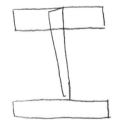

The Way I Dress

By: Shantia McNair

The Way I dress is personal but I'll give you a couple tips.

1. Get some beautiful clothes and glitter.

2. Glue the glitter to the clothes and then let it dry for about 5 to 10 minutes.

you will need clothes or shoes

Glue and glitter

11-014/015a

11-014/015b

What I like about me
is my body. I can spin
it until I get dizzy.
I can move it. I can
swallow with it. If it
hurts, I can get in bed
for a minute. It will feel
better. That's what I
like about me.

Toshua Henry

The Thing I love most about My self is the way look because it doesn't matter how big or small you are and how you look becaues most people, love you for the way you are and it doesn't matter how short or tall and it doesn't matter what you wear. Some people might not like you But that is OK !! I still love me for me!

and thas when I found a ture friend

"The privilege of having the opportunity to speak to the 3rd graders of Sarah Moore Greene Elementary School was a very uplifting experience. The kids were very interactive in the activities presented before them. In the time I spent with them, they gave me a great feeling of excitement and memories of good times. We went out to recess and they showed a lot of enthusiasm and spunk! I hope this experience will empower them to have good self-esteem and to reach out to others when in need of help. I also hope that they have faith and belief in themselves, knowing that they can accomplish any and everything in life."

—**Youth Advocate Ramel Gilliam, 21**

We have individual talents and abilities and we are proud of **what we can do.**

"The kids were all really eager and filled with joy. They were very sweet and energetic. I had so much fun with them. The teachers were also very nice. I could tell how much they care. It was a wonderful experience, and I absolutely love the kids!"

—**Youth Advocate Genesis Hardin, 18**

"This experience was amazing for me. It helped me get in touch with my inner child which I forced down and locked away many years ago. Seeing kids just be themselves, with not a care in the world, makes me wonder how they will cope with the real world. I wasn't ready for the real world, but I want them to be. I got a lot out of being there for them. I got to see that being yourself is the best solution to any situation or conflict."

—**Youth Advocate Chris Ball, 19**

My name is Parkere and what I love about myself is that I'm funny; talented; smart; and a great person. I love how I play football. I'm a great runner... I made track because I can run fast. I love how I look and how I talk too. I love my name. I love how I play basketball. I love how I dance. I love everything I do because I love me!!!

11-014/0024b-

John Cotner

I am proud that I learnedhow to ride a bike. It started win I was over my aunty house. I fell a cauple of times but I strated ride and ride and I did it and thats I learned how to ride a bike.

11-014/028

Tre' Harper 4/7/2011 HS

I am most proud of how I mayed two allstar team. I was very good at basketball. Me and Trey was very good at basketball We won all all of our basketball games. We won ten games and a rolled. We played 50 playofts games we won all of them. Very day at basketball practice I all about the tum people there. And the last pepole to live there wen Practice was over I use to do is soth annod with a friend. I use to come there ever saturday to play a game with my friend. If you do sthing you will be good at it. On saturday my step brother and I will yo down to the Y and we play a game of basketball. After we won all of are playofts games. We went to the chapion chip game lctt. we woh all of our games. After the champion chip. we be came champion. After the champion chip game After the june my team mat said good game.

What I love about myself is that I like playing baseball because I help my team. I throw the ball really well. I hit the ball hard. I do a good job running the bases. I even drink heathy stuff so it can give me more energy Baseball is my favorite sport.

K'Shindai Hobbs

I Like BaseBall Tyreque

I can run, slide, climb, cut the grass, set the bases and weed eat. I try to make 20 home runs each and every day I go to my uncle's house but I win a lot because I Play with my little cousins.

Tyreaue

What I like about my self is the way I shoot. Because I only get fouled.

By. Michael Drew

I can play basketball   James Hill

I'm good at basketball. I can dribble the ball. I can shoot the ball. I can take it between my legs. I had bounce the ball off my brothers heads. I had bounce it off my daddy's foot. I jumped off my brothers back and slamed dunked. I rolled the ball off the roof and swish in my daddy's face. I jumped off the tree and kicked the basketball. It had went over there head. Then I jumped down and did a lay up. So listen up I made it on the basketball team. I'm good at basketball.

11-014/030a

11-014/030b

What I love about myself is I Know how to run,. Faster because of my legs and how my legs go fast. And I can be faster than other people that so I can be on the falcon's Boy's Track Team and go to the UT Black Toms Track so I can get my track shirt so I can go to Ohio and race other people that are fast.

Michael Age 9

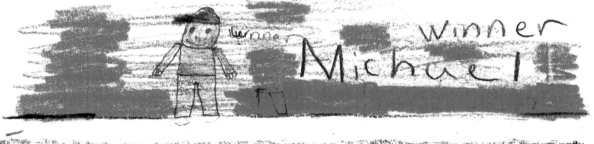

I love to play soccer. I like to play with my dog and I love to play soccer with my brother. It is fun. We sweat a lot. My parents like to play with us sometimes, too. It is good exercise.

By Cesar Tião

Hi my name is Jordan and I am going to tell you about myself I like how I play football and how I play basketball. I like that I am friendly to people, but what I love most about myself is me!
Jordan   , Age 9

How God made me

By: Asmani

I have a good imagination. Do you know how I have one? Because every time I play with my baby sister I know how to make stuff. I made a rollercoaster out of clothes baskets and wrapped blankets around chairs to make an airplane. But you still don't know thats true, so you can either ask my momma or my to sisters. I would never lie about amagination because I am a imagination.

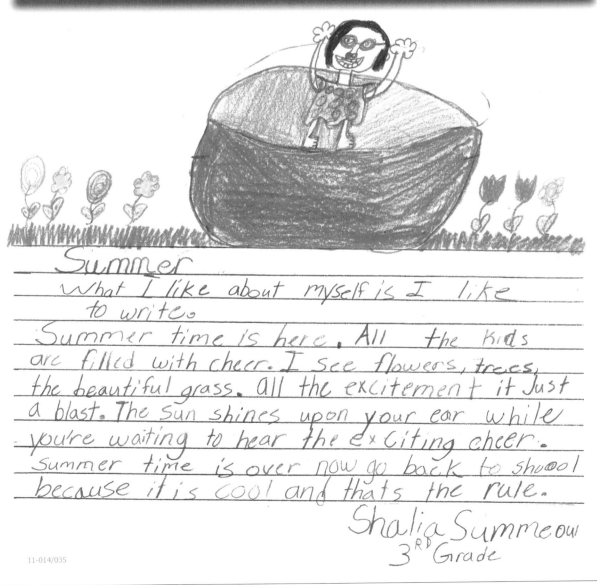

Summer

What I like about myself is I like to write.

Summer time is here. All the kids are filled with cheer. I see flowers, trees, the beautiful grass. All the excitement it Just a blast. The Sun shines upon your ear while you're waiting to hear the exciting cheer. Summer time is over now go back to school because it is cool and thats the rule.

Shalia Summeow
3ʳᵈ Grade

Roland go to The city.
I Can write but I like School
I like to walk in the wind day
with my mom walk home
School is out The Bus door is open for
Me
The Bus opens The door I walk
home it is Friday I see tv
but I go out said to The City
I Kick The can.

Roland H Douglas

SMG

Roland

11-014/037

My name is Mike.
I tie my shoes tight.
Everybody laugh at me
like I'm in a fight.

Every time when I got some Hardees
it turns out to be a realy big party.
But I got to go go to go get some moshmellows
so I can sleep on my pellow.

I got a lot of hony and
I got a lot of many
but I'm about to bee it
because I'm looking funny.

I'm at school now
we going to Motown
now we going to have fun in
the bowling aisle.

—Amauri T. Adams

Mansion

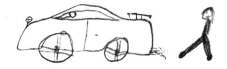

11-014/038

I Like that I am fast and I'm Creative and I Like that I can draw but Mostly I Like that I am the Littlest on my Football team and that I Like to make paper airplanes and other Crafts

I really Like Me!

Christopher Age 9

11-014/039a

Jasance Killins

Bats are mammals that live in dim caves. They eat bugs and small creatures. Bats sleep in the gentle dawn and awake in the night. They soar in the skies high and low. They have sharp fangs and little wings. They're very shy nocternal animals. Bats are very awsome animals to learn about to me. They are my favorite nocteral animal.

I love to draw and write because it is fun. It take your mad out of you. I love to make people laugh.

What I like about myself is that God gave me a talent and that is drawing. I love to draw. When I finish my homework, I draw the rest of the day. Sometimes my friends like Na'Shaune ask me for my artwork, and that's fine with me. At the Ymca people say I'm a good artist. I'm still trying to figure out if I should be an artist or football player. I love how people say can you draw this or that. That's what I like about myself.

What I like about Myself.

By: Zayna Muhammad

What I like about myself is how I write and draw. When I grow up I want to be an artist and an art teacher.

When I was in kindergarden my handwriting was only a little good, but I had good color, and first grade was the same. In the middle of the year, still in first grade, I started to try and draw more. I think I got my drawing from my mama. In second grade my teacher made us write our very best. Me and my friends always usually draw, that's when I started to love to draw. One day when I was at my nanna's house I saw a drawing book with drawings to draw inside it. My nanna let me have it. I drew a picture of a man on a horse, a turtle, a pollar bare, a glass sliper, a bee, a cat, and a bird. Sence then, I realy love to draw and write.

11-014/043

I love drawing. I like drawing better than writing. I draw cartoon people. I only draw when I am happy. I do it because it seems fun. I will always pay atention to what I am doing. I will never stop Drawing.

11-014/044

MUMMiE>

I really love my brain.
I like to Be smart, I like
to Buy a BOOK name Diary of
a wimpy kid. That Let me smart.
I like to play playground and
vedoe Game. I like to Buy
Goose bumps BOOK that scary.
And movies Diary of a wimpy kid
and I like to. Trian to track meet
is in Aplrl the 18th. So I could
Go fast and I like to dream of
I was a smart kid all time. I love
being smart and fast using my
brain.
                 Joshua Age 9

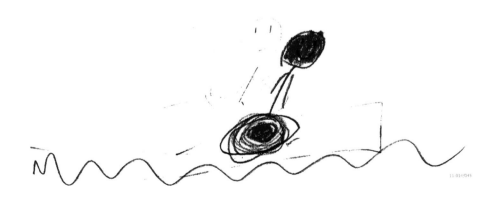

Enrique Valentine

6 1 9

Ezra A. Montella

I like myself because I can dance.
I can dance with my eyes closed.
I can dance with my arms behind
back. I can read 5th grade books. I can
read very very good. I really like
myself.

Darrion   9

What I Love is my voice. I can sing so good that I can sing a lullabye I Love my voice. sometimes I Like to sing high and low. I Can talk with it, scream with it and I can tell the truth and think with it too.

by BreshieYah Glenn

What I love about me is that I like to sing. I started singing when I was two. I start to sing when I hear a song. I will get up and dance, too. I want to grow up and be famous. I would like to be on movies and TV shows, have concerts, and have fun doing it all. I hope your dreams come true one day.

Eliza Croom

"Participating in the project brought back memories. It made me feel excited. I had fun with the students and with the teachers. I was able to share my experiences and share with them about my disability. I wanted the kids to know that it is important to stay out of trouble and how to make good choices, and to be yourself. I told the kids to believe in themselves, and to respect who they are and respect others."

—Youth Advocate Jonathan Peak, 21

We are aware of what we think and how we feel and we love who we are.

"I talked to the kids about my childhood and how I got picked on as a child. I asked the kids about their experiences and what names people call them, and their responses even hurt my feelings! I told them that no matter what, being different is a good thing. …Kids came from other classes and asked, 'Do you know what people call me?' They told me about how people teased them or made fun of them, and I replied, "You are what you answer to! You are a beautiful young lady, or a fine young man. Don't let any one tell you differently. The kids are amazing and I love them all dearly. …Dealing with the kids was an eye opener because all of them were so different. It's amazing how quickly kids will open up to you. When you pay attention and show them that you care, they will open up like blossoming flowers."

—Youth Advocate Aneja Raiteri, 19

I like myself because I'm beautiful. I like myself because I have many friends and they are thoughtful and kind I like myself because I'm special my brother's and sisters hate it when I get all the attention. I love myself because I have a family and I wasn't left on the street. When I grow up I want to be a teacher I like myself because I can run fast and I go to church to learn the word I Love my Family.

Karrington Age 9

How Do You Love yourself

Pation Loves Grace

by Trinity Elaine Turner

I have heart and Soul I Love You family

Who and what I live for.

I live for my family and me, and I Live a life so sweet. When my family goes on vacation its always fun, but when they make me laugh I can't get enough.

I Love my life, and This is Who and What I Live for.

11-014/053

⭐ I Love my family and my friend ⭐

My family says I look like my mama. I do and I love my family. I'm thankful for the things they get me and I am happy that I have a family! I love my family and my friends Jetorl, Kyla, Zayna, and Mariah. Thank you my friends for being there for me. I love a of y'all.

By: Sheli'yah Bradley

Me and my sister have lots of adventures but then she cries and I ask her why. She says I love you you love me too, little sis. we go to the park and have a picnic and go to the swing. she tells me that she loves me and I say I love you to.

By: Amaya Tarver

The look alike famliy
by Mariah Smith

That everybody said I look like
everybody in my famliy. Like my
brother, sister, grandma, grandpa,
mom, dad, stepdad, puppy, uncle,
aunty, stepsisters, cousins, friends,
and some of my toys. Sometimes
I feel shy, sweet, and kind.
I always feel special when
somebody says that. I have this
feeling that's kind of like butterflies
in my stomach. It tickles and
I kind of like it.

I like my mommy
dog and my cats Gracie
and a beakers. I like
me for me.

Jayda Pittman

Jayda Pittman

44

I am proud to have a teacher that can teach me new things that I as a child don't know. And I am proud to have family and friends that care about me. But most of all my body is what allows me to go to new levels. I just want to say thank you God for letting me see another day. I am very grateful for what you have done to me. And I just want to say thank you everyone who supported me to get where I am now.

—**JeTori Howard**

What I like about myself is God created me in his own image and that is good. I'm funny. I share things with other people.

—**Jaylin Dixon**

I love everyone and you should, too. It doesn't matter what color they are, what they do, or what they look like. I love enemies, friends, neighbors, and family. God brought us here for one reason and that reason is to love others!

—**Rachel Bradley**

I love the way I look because that's the way God made me and I love it. I love it because my family loves me. I love me, too. So I am going to teach you how to love yourself like I learned. First, do people say you have a big head? Well if they do, don't feel bad. People used to say that to me, too. People called me big ears. I'm going to teach you how to ignore them, because if you ignore them they will leave you alone. If they keep hurting your feelings just ask God or Jesus to help you.

—**Iyouna Smith**

Hi. My name is Da'Nea Pendergrass. I'm going to tell you about myself. What I love or like about myself is that I love the way I help people when they are feeling down. I like how I'm helpful to my parents. I love how I get excellent grades and how I'm awesome at math. I love that I'm a Star Student because I am a good girl. I like how people shine. That is why I love and like me!

—**Da'Nea Pendergrass**

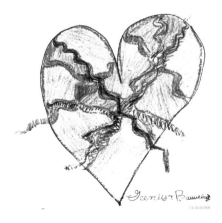

What I love

about myself is my heart because it is full of love and secrets. It is an important part of my body. I love my heart because it makes me shine so brightly.

—**Geniya Bawling**

I help people by

taking out the trash and I mop the floor. When I get finished I wash the dishes. So then I get to clean my room and clean my closet. I use Windex™ for the windows. When I get finished I get to wash my dad's truck and his car. When get I finished with that I sweep the floors. I love to work for other people.

—**James Elliott**

We all love each

other. You and I we love each other so very much. We do everything together. We both wear our hair the same. I love you and you love me. Just come on and me and you can have a great time. If we clear our mind and think of something good and keep our minds to it, then we can be best friends forever.

—**Skydaisha Miller**

The things I like

about myself are that I'm caring for others and helpful. My Grandma and I feed homeless people. We also take care of them and we get them homes. I think that I'm amazing to some people that don't get on my nerves. Sometimes I can be helpful to people that I don't know. I'm kind to others. This is what I learned, "If you help or are joyful to someone they will do the same." I also like that my mom got her GED and now my mom is a nurse. I like the way I sing and play basketball. I love myself!

—**Kiava Watson**

What about yourself

are you most proud of? I can make friends. I am funny. I have cheerful friends. When I was sad my friends helped me to get better. When someone was sad I helped them and we became friends. When me and JaMican were at my dad's job and I was sad because my dad was in the Army, JaMican played with me. JaMican is my funny cousin.

—**Marcus Alford**

I love how I look. I'm

pretty. I love how I'm very, very, very funny. I love how I draw. I love how I act and how I look different. I love how I do things. I love all

By: Skydaisha Miller

11-014/060

my drawings. They are very creative. I love how I play every day. I like how I share with my mom, my friends, with my granny, with my brother. I love to think.

— **Cindy Jackson**

What I love about
myself is that I am a smart girl. I don't need anybody talking about me. I know I am a beautiful girl. I know what's wrong and right. I know I can do better.

—**Treliyah Jackson**

...I sing good. I love
me for how I am. I love my mommy and daddy. I love my teacher. I love my school! I love me.

—**Madison Craine**

What I like about
me is when I believe something, nobody can take my beliefs away. That is a good thing. Some people believe different things. It is okay, too. I think nobody should be judged about what they believe because you would not want anybody to judge you. That is what I like about me.

—**Destin Thomas**

CPSIA information can be obtained
at www.ICGtesting.com
Printed in the USA
237660LV00001BD